grandma

tell me your story

Your childhood

To be born is not to come into the world. To be born is to come into life.

MICHEL HENRY

Paste your photo here representing you as a child

The day of your birth: date, place, anecdote

...

_____
_____
_____
_____
_____
_____
_____
_____

What is the name of your parents? What is the story of their meeting?

_____
_____
_____
_____
_____
_____

Do you have brothers and / or sisters? Write their first names, date of birth and note their main character traits. If not, would you have liked to have some? Explain me why.

___

Do you have a particular distinctive sign? Describe yourself physically.

___

What is the origin of your first name? Why did your parents call you like that?

___

Do you have any nicknames?

_____
_____
_____
_____
_____
_____
_____
_____

What is the anecdote that you do not remember but that you were told from your childhood and that marked you?

_____
_____
_____
_____
_____
_____
_____
_____
_____

What is the anecdote of your childhood that you remember this time that marked you?

_____
_____
_____
_____
_____
_____
_____
_____

Tell me about the house (or houses) where you grew up, the neighbors, the surroundings

What kind of student were you at school? What were your passions? Your dreams ?

※ Who were your best friends? Do you still see them?

※ Did you have any animals? If so, what were their names?

★ What did you want to do for a job later?

★ *Did you often go on vacation? Or this ? Tell me about a summer memory!*

※ What is your fondest childhood memory?

※ What is your worst childhood memory?

★ What was your favorite dish made by your parents? By your grandparents?

★ What is your biggest physical injury as a child and how did it happen?

What did you learn from life during your childhood that you would like to pass on to me?

Tell me your most beautiful christmas keepsake

your preferences

FAVORITE FILM FROM YOUR CHILDHOOD

FAVORITE MUSIC FROM YOUR CHILDHOOD

PREFERRED MEAL (Starter + main course + dessert)

FAVORITE ACTIVITY

MADELEINE DE PROUST

free space to write what you want

things to do in childhood

1.
2.
3.
4.
5.
6.
7.
8.
9.
10.

things to do in childhood

1.
2.
3.
4.
5.
6.
7.
8.
9.
10.

Tell me the story of our family

Draw our family tree here

Draw our Family tree here

Your Adolescence

Adolescence is the only time you have learned anything.

Paste your photo here of your teenage period

MARCELPROUST

* How did you dress? What was your style?

___

* What were the conflicts with your parents?

___

✦ Tell me how you lived your adolescence with anecdotes

✦ *Tell me your funniest memory from that time*

※ Tell me about your first kiss

※ *Tell me about your first love*

※ What was your greatest pain?

※ *If it wasn't heartache, tell me how you experienced your first heartache*

⭒ Were you complexed by your physique? Do you like boys?

⭒ What was the craziest thing you've done as a teenager?

※ Did you do things you weren't proud of when you were a teenager?

※ *What events (political, cultural or other) marked you during this period?*

★ What were your fears? Your apprehensions? Do they still exist today?

★ *What did you learn in class that you still remember?*

★ What is your best memory in middle school / high school?

_____
_____
_____
_____
_____
_____
_____
_____
_____
_____
_____
_____
_____
_____
_____

★ Conversely, your worst memory in college / high school?

_____
_____
_____
_____
_____
_____
_____
_____
_____
_____
_____
_____
_____
_____
_____

※ What is your best teenage vacation?

※ What is your worst teenage vacation?

※ Tell me about the most embarrassing memory

※ What were your hobbies? Have you won any competitions, contests?

your preferences

Favorite film from your teenage

FAVORITE MUSIC FROM YOUR teenage

PREFERRED MEAL (Starter + main course + dessert)

Favorite activity

madeleine of proust

free space to write what you want

TOP 10 OF
advice To cross
adolisence

1.

2.

3.

4.

5.

6.

7.

8.

9.

10.

Top 10 of
eurors not to be reproduced

1.

2.

3.

4.

5.

6.

7.

8.

9.

10.

Adult life

Adulthood is the proper age of adaptation. To mature is to find your place in the world.

EMMAN UELMO UNIER

Your photo

* Did you do any higher education?
_____
_____
_____
_____
_____
_____
_____
_____

* What profession (s) did you exercise?
_____
_____
_____
_____
_____
_____
_____
_____

What was your greatest joy?

What was your greatest pain?

What is the biggest difficulty you encountered and how did you overcome it?

Describe to me your work, what you liked or didn't like

※ How did you meet my grandfather? Tell me your story!

※ *Have you had one or more animals during your adult life?*

※ At what age did you become a mom? Why did you decide to have one or more children?

※ How did you choose the first names of your children?

✳ Have you traveled a lot? Tell me about your best trip!

✳ *What is the most surprising thing you have seen / heard in your adult life*

✸ What is the meeting that impressed you the most besides someone you fell in love with?

✸ When did you really become an adult?

What are the lessons of your adult life that you would like to pass on to me?

your preferences

FAVORITE FILM FROM YOUR ADULT

[   ]

FAVORITE MUSIC FROM YOUR adult

[   ]

PREFERRED MEAL (Starter + main course + dessert)

[   ]

FAVORITE ACTIVITY

[   ]

MADELEINE DE PROUST

[   ]

free space to write what you want

[   ]

TOP 10 OF
advice on becoming an adult

1.
2.
3.
4.
5.
6.
7.
8.
9.
10.

pitfalls to avoid

1.

2.

3.

4.

5.

6.

7.

8.

9.

10.

Your old days

If youth knew, if old age could.

Paste your photo here of the adult age

HENRI ESTIENNE

※ How do you feel being retired?

_____
_____
_____
_____
_____
_____
_____
_____
_____

※ *Is it hard to grow old? What are the + points and the - points?*

_____
_____
_____
_____
_____
_____
_____

✳ Do you have any regrets?

✳ Do you have remorse?

★ What do you do of your days ? What are your hobbies ?

★ *Do you still believe in love?*

What is your fondest memory in all years?

Are there any thoughts you had when you were young about older people that make you think you were young and dumb today?

Have you kept a secret all your life that you would like to reveal to me now?

Do you believe in the afterlife?

- If you were to die today, how would you like your funeral to go? What would you like to wear? What would you like us to do?

- Where would you like to spend your old age ideally?

✳ Have you found meaning in life after all these years?

✳ What did old age teach you after all?

your prefernces as a grandmather

MATURITY'S FAVORITE FILM

MATURITY'S FAVORITE MUSIC

PREFERRED MEAL (Starter + main course + dessert)

ACTIVITÉ PRÉFÉRÉE

THE PERSON YOU MISS MOST

Free space to write whatever you want

TOP 10 OF
things to do before it's too late

1.

2.

3.

4.

5.

6.

7.

8.

9.

10.

REGRETS OF YOUR LIFE

1.
2.
3.
4.
5.
6.
7.
8.
9.
10.

FAMILY RECIPE

INGREDIENTS

Name of recipe

FOR HOW MUCH

preparation time

COOKING TIME

INSTRUCTIONS

NOTES

FAMILY RECIPE

INGREDIENTS

Name of recipe

FOR HOW MUCH

preparation time

COOKING TIME

INSTRUCTIONS

NOTES

FAMILY RECIPE

INGREDIENTS

Name of recipe

FOR HOW MUCH

preparation time

COOKING TIME

NOTES

INSTRUCTIONS

FAMILY RECIPE

INGREDIENTS

Name of recipe

FOR HOW MUCH

preparation time

COOKING TIME

NOTES

INSTRUCTIONS

FAMILY RECIPE

INGREDIENTS

Name of recipe

FOR HOW MUCH

preparation time

COOKING TIME

INSTRUCTIONS

NOTES

FAMILY RECIPE

INGREDIENTS

Name of recipe

FOR HOW MUCH

preparation time

COOKING TIME

NOTES

INSTRUCTIONS

FAMILY RECIPE

INGREDIENTS

Name of recipe

FOR HOW MUCH

preparation time

COOKING TIME

NOTES

INSTRUCTIONS

FAMILY RECIPE

INGREDIENTS

Name of recipe

FOR HOW MUCH

preparation time

COOKING TIME

INSTRUCTIONS

NOTES

FAMILY RECIPE

Name of recipe

FOR HOW MUCH

preparation time

COOKING TIME

NOTES

INGREDIENTS

INSTRUCTIONS

Your favorite books

tell me what to slice them for

BOOK 01	
BOOK 02	
BOOK 03	
BOOK 04	
BOOK 05	

Your favorite works of art

tell me what you love him for

ART 01	
ART 02	
ART 03	
ART 04	
ART 05	

Your favorite smells

tell me what you love him for

ODOR 01	
ODOR 02	
ODOR 03	
ODOR 04	
ODOR 05	

Your favorite landscapes
tell me what you love him for

VIEW 01	
VIEW 02	
VIEW 03	
VIEW 04	
VIEW 05	

Your favorite quotes

tell me what you love him for

DIXIT 01

DIXIT 02

DIXIT 03

DIXIT 04

DIXIT 05

Your favorite films

tell me what you love him for

FILM 01	
FILM 02	
FILM 03	
FILM 04	
FILM 05	

DATE :

Letter to my grandchildren

DATE:

Letter to my grandchildren

Glue an unforgettable photo

Glue an unforgettable photo

Glue an unforgettable photo

Glue an unforgettable photo

Glue an unforgettable photo

Glue an unforgettable photo

Glue an unforgettable photo

Free space for creation

Free space for creation

Free space for creation

Free space for creation

Free space for creation

Free space for creation

Free space for creation

Free space for creation

Free space for creation

Free space for creation

Free space for creation

Free space for creation

Free space for creation

Free space for creation

Free space for creation

Free space for creation

Free space for creation

www.ingramcontent.com/pod-product-compliance
Lightning Source LLC
LaVergne TN
LVHW010351191224
799473LV00038B/1206